QATAR 2022

FANS FAVORITE

TRAVEL GUIDE

Contents

TOURIST OFFICES
WHERE TO STAY
QATAR FOODS AND DRINKS

QATAR HISTORY, LANGUAGE AND CULTURE
GETTING AROUND QATAR
WORLD CUP STADIUMS

James CAMERON

Qatar 2022

Fans Favorite Travel Guide

James CAMERON

Contents

Copyright

About Qatar

The eyes of the world are on Qatar right now.

This little Gulf state was transformed from a modest fishing and commerce hub to one of the richest (per capita) nations in the world following the discovery of oil in the 1940s.

Qatar is expanding at an incredible rate because of its oil and natural gas revenues. The desert floor is overrun with everything from colleges to commercial centres, five-star hotels to football stadiums.

Modern Qatar is a city-state. The area surrounding Doha, the nation's capital, is home to more than half of the population. Between oil fields, which are Qatar's main source of riches, are other communities and "districts." Beyond all other aspects, the nation has its fair share of natural beauty, with stunning beaches lining the western coast and breathtaking dunes encircling Khor Al Adaid in the south. Additionally, the large Al Thakira mangroves at Al Khor on the eastern seaboard offer a striking contrast to the nearby desert environment.

Although Islam is the most common religion in Qatar, the country's culture is remarkably tolerant. Foreigners' civil liberties are respected, and they are free to practice different religions. Additionally, there is a lot of press freedom in the area.

Qatar has not forgotten its deeply established religious and cultural history while advancing toward openness. Only hotel bars and restaurants serve alcohol, work schedules are heavily influenced by religious holidays like

Ramadan, and traditional activities like falconry and camel racing are still favoured in past times. Qatar is a complex but beautiful country, much like the geometrically patterned Islamic art that can be found throughout the place.

Key facts

Area: 11,627 sq km (4,489 sq miles)

Population density: 2,788,000 (2019)

Capital: Doha

Government: Emirate

Head of state: Amir Sheikh Tamim bin Hamad Al Thani since 2013

Head of government: Prime minister Sheikh Khalid bin Khalifa bin Abdul Aziz Al Thani since 2020

Qatar History, Language and Culture

History of Qatar

Many Qataris relied on commerce and pearl-fishing for their livelihood before the discovery of oil and natural gas.

Qatar formally became a British protectorate in 1916 after the two countries signed a contract. Oil was found in Dukhan in 1940, and once commercial production began in 1949, the nation grew wealthy. In 1968, Qatar briefly merged with other little Gulf states to form the United Arab Emirates, but it quickly withdrew and declared independence on September 3, 1971. After gaining its independence, Qatar sponsored Al Jazeera, a television network renowned for its unbiased news coverage, to encourage political openness. Additionally, a sizable US military base is located there. However, due to Qatar's suspected support for violent Islamist groups (including the Muslim Brotherhood) and its cordial ties with Iran, its relations with its neighbours, particularly Saudi Arabia, Bahrain, and the United Arab Emirates, have become tense recently. Saudi Arabia, the United Arab Emirates, Bahrain, and Egypt severed diplomatic ties with Qatar in 2017 and enacted an economic boycott.

Did you know:

- There is a blue road in Qatar. Abdullah Bin Jassim Street near Souq Waqif is painted blue, instead of the usual black asphalt. Apart from being pleasing to the eye, the blue colour absorbs and radiates less heat, making the road cooler too.

- Camel racing is one of the popular sports in Qatar. During races, the camel jockeys are robots placed atop the camel, remotely controlled by the camel owners.

- Qatar funds the Al Jazeera Media Network, known for its independent news coverage.

Qatar culture

Religion in Qatar

About 95% of Qataris are Sunni Muslims

Social Conventions in Qatar

As in every other nation, it is crucial to follow customs and etiquette. Visitors shouldn't dress provocatively in public locations, both men and women. By the hotel pool, beachwear and bikinis are permissible, but not in public.

Men shake hands to begin business meetings, and titles like "Sheikh" or "Haji" should be used to convey respect. The small conversation is typical and used to develop relationships. Never bring business matters in a hurry.

When meeting someone for the first time, business cards are frequently exchanged. Take a moment to read the card you receive because it is considered impolite to put it away before reading it. Your name card should ideally be printed in Arabic on one side.

Languages in Qatar

Arabic is the official language. English is widely spoken.

Qatar Weather, Climate and geography

Weather and climate

Best time to visit

The sovereign state of Qatar, which is located on a small piece of land along the eastern coast of the Arabian Peninsula, has a dry, subtropical desert climate with little annual precipitation and extremely hot and muggy summers.

The two main seasons in Qatar are hot (May to October) and cool (November to April). The transitional months of March, April, and November feature hot but comfortable temperatures.

Qatar is at its most pleasant between December and February when average high temperatures range from 22 °C (72 °F) to 25 °C. With temperatures ranging from 14OC (57oF) to 22OC, January is the coolest month. The average maximum temperature returns to 29°C in March after temperatures begin to rise in February. November and March are the ideal times to visit too if you like warmer temperatures.

Although the cool season is the best time to visit Qatar, keep in mind that rainfall, albeit infrequent, does happen then as well. It mostly happens in the form of strong cloudbursts and thunderstorms.

It is better to stay out of the hot season (May to October). Although it's not uncommon for a thermometer to reach an eye-watering high of 50OC

(122oF) in July and occasionally August, July is frequently regarded as the hottest month with temperatures ranging from 32oC (90oF) to 43oC (109oF). You might find yourself looking for shelter in one of the many air-conditioned malls if you visit during the hot season. Things tend to drop off after October, and by November, you can anticipate an average high of 30 degrees Celsius.

Even though coastal locations may be a little cooler than inland due to Qatar's small size and flat terrain, there is little regional weather difference. Due to Doha's dense urbanization, the city's temperature may appear to be a little hotter than it is.

Required clothing

All year long, cotton and linen that is lightweight are suggested. While a jacket is a need for cooler evenings throughout the cool season, a cardigan is useful for cooled malls. If you want to go camping between January and March, you'll be glad you brought an additional layer of clothes for the evenings.

Abayas and head scarves are optional for female guests, although loose-fitting cotton gowns that cover your shoulders and knees are preferred. Avoid wearing anything too tight or exposed. Men ought to dress modestly as well. Be aware that while bikinis and beachwear are permitted at the hotel pool, they are not permitted in public areas.

Geography

The Qatar peninsula spans roughly 80 kilometres (50 miles) from east to west and 160 kilometres (99 miles) from north to south. Although the country is largely made up of low-lying desert, its centre contains an elevated limestone plateau. In Qatar, there are no freshwater rivers or lakes.

There is a sizable tract of mangroves close to Al Khor on Qatar's northeastern coast. As it moves closer to the southeastern edge, the coastline gradually changes into large sabha (salt flats). Khor Al Adaid, which translates to "inland sea," is where the sea, together with the nearby sizable tidal embayment, spills into the desert in the south of the nation, forming a distinctive scenery.

On the northern side of the country, there are small pockets of agricultural lands used for growing dates, along with some vegetable patches.

On the west coast of Qatar lies the Dukhan field, the country's main oil field. Geographically, several small hills are stretching from Dukhan towards the border with Saudi Arabia.

Qatar: Doing business and staying in touch

Doing business in Qatar

The secret to a successful business encounter is politeness and patience. Before moving on to business topics in a second encounter, a first meeting may well concentrate more on polite, personal queries about family, travel plans, etc. When meeting a Qatari business associate for the first time, it is traditional to exchange gifts. Though it's a common choice, traditional perfume should never contain alcohol.

Office hours

Sunday to Thursday 07:00 - 15:30. Government offices work between 07:00 – 14:00. Hours may be reduced during the holy month of Ramadan.

Economy

Qatar has thrived despite the world's struggling economies, consistently ranking among the top three nations in terms of GDP per capita.

While the climate and water availability hamper agriculture, the Qatari government has increased its oil and natural gas income while attempting to diversify through industrialization.

GDP

US$191.4 billion (2018)

Main exports

Oil and gas.

Main imports

Consumer goods, machinery and food.

Main trading partners

The USA, China, Germany, and Japan.

Keeping in touch in Qatar

Telephone

There are no area codes

Mobile Phone

Roaming agreements exist with most international mobile phone operators. Network coverage across the country is excellent.

Internet

Wi-fi is widely available.

Media

The Qatari media industry is most famous for the TV News channel Al-Jazeera. Which launched in 1996.

Post

Airmail to Europe takes up to one week.

Post office hours

Sunday – Thursday 07:00 – 19:00, Saturday 08:00 – 11:00 and 17:00 – 20:00

Travel to Qatar

Flying to Qatar

Qatar Airways (www.qatarairways.com) is the national airline, linking Qatar to over 160 international destinations. Other airlines that fly to Qatar include Air India, Astana, British Airways, and Cathay Pacific. Ethiopian Airlines, among others.

The major airport is Doha Hamad International Airport.

Airport guides

Doha Hamad International Airport.

Location

The airport is located around 9km (5.6miles) southeast of central Doha.

Telephone

+97440106666

Address

Doha Hamad International Airport.

Flight times

From London – 6 hours 45 minutes; New York – 12 hours 20 minutes, Sydney – 15 hours 10 minutes, Singapore – 7 hours 40 minutes.

Departure tax

None

Travelling to Qatar by rail

At present, there are no passenger rail services to Qatar from Saudi Arabia, the only country with which Qatar shares its land borders.

Driving to Qatar

Qatar shares land borders with Saudi Arabia which may be shut from time to time due to conflicts. Even when the borders are opened, only residents of Qatar, Saudi Arabia and UAE along with permit holders, can cross the borders.

GETTING TO QATAR BY BOAT

Doha and Ras Laffan are the main ports. The water traffic is mostly commercial.

Cruise ships

Some cruise lines like MSC Cruises (www. MSC cruises, com) include Doha on their Middle Eastern itineraries.

Where to stay in Qatar

Hotels

1

Grading: Hotels are graded from 1-5

Camping

Many tour operators organize overnight camping in the desert near Khor Al Adair. With kebabs spitting over the fire, stars spangling the sky and the dulcet voice of your guide intoning Arabic poetry, this can be a highlight of a trip to Qatar.

While you are there

Things to see and do in Qatar

Attractions in Qatar

AL Khor

Al Kohr, which is 50 kilometres (31 miles) northeast of Doha, has a very relaxed environment. It features lovely beaches, a zoo in a family park, and Qatar's largest dairy farm, which has a petting zoo, a playground, an obstacle course, and a place for horseback riding.

Al Zubarah

Al Zubarah is 104 kilometres (65 miles) northwest of Doha. Al Zubarah, a UNESCO World Heritage Site, was once a major pearl fishing and trading harbour and is now a superb illustration of a Gulf merchant town from the 18th and 19th centuries. The Al Zubarah Fort is the main attraction here.

Dahl Al Misfir Cave

This 40m (131ft) deep cave is a geological marvel made primarily of fibrous gypsum, which is phosphorescent, or able to emit a faint glow when exposed to ultraviolet light. The cave is located 25 miles (40 km) west of Doha.

Doha

Doha, the cultural and commercial centre of Qatar, is where most tourists arrive and set up shop. The Corniche, a 7 km (4 mi) long seaside promenade in Doha, is a well-liked destination for tourists. The Corniche, which stretches from the Sheraton Hotel to the Museum of Islamic Art, offers stunning views, spacious green spaces, and a harbour where you may go on a dhow cruise.

Doha, Katara

Katara, a purpose-built cultural centre, presents numerous performances, plays, and exhibitions all year round. Along with eateries, cafes, markets, and a well-kept public beach with water sports, there is also one.

Doha, Museum of Islamic Art

The exquisitely designed museum by I. M. Pel has established itself as a landmark in Doha. The interior of the building is spacious and light, and the collection of artwork, glassworks, fabrics, manuscripts, and ceramics is spectacular. Give yourself lots of time to wander. The on-site three Michelin-starred restaurants are certainly worthwhile a visit, and the outdoor patio is ideal for a drink in the evening.

Doha, Souq Waqif

Try out your negotiating skills with the traders in Souq Waqif, where you can discover top-quality Middle Eastern goods like spices and perfumes. A traditional falconry market, a visitor centre with cultural performances, and a variety of restaurants are all located inside. If you don't want to shop, grab a coffee and sit down to people-watch.

The desert

The sand desert in Qatar offers breathtaking sunrises and beautiful, starry skies at night. The dunes can also be traversed in a 4x4, a quad, or even a surfboard.

The desert, Khor Al Adair

The impressive Khor Al Adair, also known as the "inland sea," is located 60 kilometres (37 miles) southeast of Doha. Here, the sea and a sizable tidal embayment spill into the desert. A wide variety of plants and animals can be found here. It is best to reserve an overnight tour so that you can take in the magnificent sunset and sunrise.

Tourist offices

Qatar shopping and nightlife

Shopping in Qatar

Unquestionably, Doha's vast malls show a strong culture of purchasing. The Villagio mall on Al Waab street is the best place to shop for high-end clothing. Gondola rides, an IMAX theatre, and an ice rink are also available here. Another sizable building with both western and Arabic chains is the city centre mall on Fourth Street.

Souq Waqif, the main market in Doha, is most likely the greatest location to find mementoes and local delicacies. Carpets, Bedouin, weaving, Arabic coffee pots, incense burners, prayer beads, as well as local artwork and handicrafts, are examples of items that make excellent presents. It is worthwhile to visit this area for its many eateries and coffee shops even if you don't enjoy shopping.

Shopping hours

Generally Sat-Thu 1000 to1200 and 1600 to 2000 or later. Some major malls operate from 1000 to 2200 daily but have a prayer break between 1100-1300 on Friday.

Nightlife in Qatar

Many of Doha's luxury hotels also act as nightlife venues. Crystal Lounge at Doha is the hippest place. For something mellower, the Lincoln Centre at St Regis and the jazz club at Rotana are top choices. The Katara Cultural Villages (www.katara.net) also hosts concerts, shows, exhibitions, as well as indoor and outdoor film screenings.

Qatar Food and Drink

There are several high-quality dining alternatives in Doha, especially in five-star hotels. You may find a range of restaurants with Middle Eastern themes in Souq Waqif, making it a great place to eat.

The most important meal for the majority of ex-pats and tourists is brunch, especially on Friday and Saturday when hotels compete to offer the most extensive and varied menu. Any of the five-star hotels require advanced reservations.

Qatari cuisine is surprisingly diverse, including influences from the Indian Subcontinent, Iran, the Levant, and North Africa, even though the majority of product is imported from elsewhere. Usually, there are several side dishes to go with the main entrée. When it comes to dessert, locally grown dates, fresh fruit and halwa (flour-based or nut-based dessert) or Umm Ali (similar to a bread pudding) are excellent choices.

Khaleeji dish

Specialities

- *Kousa Mahshi* (stuffed zucchini)

- *Machboos* (said to be the national dish of Qatar, this slow-cooked mutton or seafood served with yoghurt dish is delicious)
- *Thread* (lamb stew made with pieces of bread, usually Raqaq or Khobez)
- *Ghazi* (a whole roast lamb served over a bed of rice and nuts)
- *Umm Ali* (bread pudding with nuts and raisins)
- *Meghalaya* (rose water and pistachio pudding)

Things to know

Alcohol is available in most top-end restaurants and hotel bars in Doha. Drinking alcohol in public outside these establishments is prohibited.

Tipping

A service charge is often added to bills in hotels and most restaurants, otherwise, 10% is appropriate.

Regional drinks

In Qatar, coffee may be the most widely consumed beverage. Small cups of coffee may be served with dates or with sugar to sweeten it. Black tea flavoured with crushed cardamom and sweetened with evaporated milk is also well-liked as Karak Chai.

The majority of restaurants offer delicious fresh juices. Both karkadeh (hibiscus tea) and limonene (a lemon and mint beverage) are quite cooling.

Getting Around Qatar

Air

Doha has Qatar’s only international airport and there are no internal flights.

Road

It is simpler to travel about Qatar by car due to its size, which is only 160 km (99 miles) from north to south and 80 km (50 miles) from east to west.

most routes branch out from the city, of Doha. There is even a "blue road" in Doha, which is Abdullah Bin Jassim Street near Souq Waqif, which is painted blue rather than black asphalt. In addition to being aesthetically beautiful, the colour blue also keeps the road cooler since it absorbs and reflects less heat.

Side of the road

Right

Road quality

It's a delight to drive on Qatar's well-maintained roadways. But watch out for speed traps. Sandstorms and flash floods both have the potential to significantly decrease visibility.

Driving in Doha may be difficult due to traffic congestion and impatient motorists.

Road Classification

Major routes are multiple-lane highways.

Car Hire

accessible at hotels and airports from national and international businesses. Although certain car rental businesses may insist that drivers be at least 21 years old, the legal driving age in Qatar is 18. One needs to use a seatbelt. Anyone caught driving without a license or without wearing a license is subject to significant on-the-spot fines.

Taxi

Karwa taxis are widely available and reasonably priced. You can order it via the app or call for service (+974 4458 8888). You can also hire a private vehicle through apps like Careem and Uber.

Bike

There are a few bike rental shops in Doha, and cycling is gaining some popularity there. Despite this, very few tourists enjoy cycling because they aren't accustomed to the hot, dry weather like the locals are.

Coach

Mowasalat (www.mowasalat.com) runs a public bus service from Doha to major towns within Qatar.

Regulations

On highways, the speed limit is 120kph (75mph). Within the city, the speed limit varies but most of the time is 60kph (37mph).

Breakdown services

There is no national breakdown service but private companies do operate. If you're renting a car, the rental company usually gives you a number to call.

Documentation

Some nationals, such as those from the UK and Canada, are permitted to drive for up to a week using their home country's license before needing an IDP (for up to 12 months). The driver's license must be carried at all times.

Rail

There are three lines in Doha's metro system: Red, Green, and Gold. From Lusail (in the north) to Al Wakra, the Red Line travels (in the south). The city centre and Terminal 1 of Hamad International Airport are also connected by this line. Al Mansoura (in the east) to Al Riffa are connected by the Green Line (in the west). The Gold Line connects Al Aziziyah to Ras Bu Abboud (in the east) (in the west).

Rail Passes

If you would like to travel on the metro regularly, you can buy different passes (Gold, Standard or Limited Use) depending on your preference.

Qatar Visa and Passport Requirements

	Passport required	Return ticket required	Visa required
British	Yes	Yes	No
EU	Yes	Yes	No
USA	Yes	Yes	No
Canadian	Yes	Yes	No
Australian	Yes	Yes	No

Passports

To enter Qatar, passports must have one blank page and be valid for at least 6 months.

Passport Note

Israeli passport holders are not permitted to enter Qatar.

Visas

In the Middle East, Qatar is the most liberal nation, granting visa-free entry to nationals of more than 90 other nations. On arrival, a visa waiver is granted upon presentation of a valid passport with a minimum remaining validity of six months, a confirmed onward or return ticket, and, if necessary, a hotel reservation that is valid for the duration of the anticipated stay in Qatar.

Antigua and Barbuda, Argentina, Austria, Bahamas, Belgium, Bulgaria, Croatia, Cyprus, Czech Republic, Denmark, Dominican Republic, Estonia, Finland, France, Germany, Greece, Hungary, Iceland, Italy, Latvia, Liechtenstein, Lithuania, Luxembourg, Malaysia, Malta, Netherlands, Norway, Poland, Portugal, Romania, Serbia, Seychelles, Slovakia, Slovenia, Spain, Sweden, Switzerland,

Nationals of the following nations are permitted to travel to Qatar and remain up to 3 days, with the possibility of an additional 30 days' waiver: The following countries are included in the list: Andorra, Australia, Azerbaijan, Belarus, Bolivia, Brazil, Brunei, Canada, Chile, China, Colombia, Costa Rica, Cuba, Ecuador, Falkland Island, French Guiana, Guyana, Hong Kong, India, Indonesia, Ireland, Japan, Kazakhstan, Lebanon, Macau, Macedonia, Maldives, Mauritius, Mexico, Moldova, Monaco, Montenegro, New Zealand, Pakistan, Panama, Paraguay,

Pakistan: Pakistani nationals are not required to obtain a visa to enter Qatar for up to 30 days as long as they have a valid credit card, a passport that is valid for at least six months, a confirmed round-trip ticket, a confirmed hotel reservation, and proof of polio immunization (if travelling directly from Pakistan).

Additionally, visitors from 37 nations who are going to Qatar and Oman can obtain a joint tourist visa when they arrive. Andorra, Australia, Austria, Belgium, Brunei, Canada, Cyprus, Denmark, Finland, France, Germany, Greece, Hong Kong, Hungary, Iceland, Ireland, Italy, Japan, Liechtenstein, Luxembourg, Malaysia, Monaco, Montenegro, Netherlands, New Zealand, Norway, Poland, Portugal, San Marino, Singapore, South Korea, Spain, Sweden, Switzerland, United Kingdom, United States, and the Vatican City are the nations in question.

You can apply for a free Electronic Travel Authorization online if you are from a nation not on the list above and you have a valid resident permit or visit visa for Australia, Canada, New Zealand, the Schengen Countries, the United Kingdom, or the United States. You are permitted to travel to Qatar for a maximum of 30 days, with a potential extension of another 30 days.

The following details must be provided on the ETA application:

Evidence of lodging in Qatar (hotel reservation or host's address)

Specifics of your departure or subsequent travel

A copy of your passport (with a minimum validity of six months)

A copy of your residence permit or visa to any one of the eligible countries stated above (with a minimum validity of 30 days)

If you are from a country not listed above and need a visa to Qatar, you can apply for it online. The cost is QAR100.

Types and Cost

Tourist visa: QAR100

Validity

Visa-free entry: varying allowable lengths of stay.

Electronic Travel Authorisation: 30 days

Tourist visa: varying allowable lengths of stay

Transit

No visa is required if you don't leave the transit area. If you do plan to leave the airport, a transit visa is available for 24 hours.

Application

Visit https://portal.moi.gov.qa/qatarvisas/

Temporary residence

You can only apply for a temporary residence visa if you have a firm job offer or contract from an employer in Qatar. Work permits can only be obtained by a local sponsor.

Entry with pets

You must obtain a permit from the Department of Animal Resources, along with a health certificate issued by a vet in your home country.

Embassies and tourist offices

Embassy or the State of Qatar in the USA

Telephone: +1 202 274 1600

Website:

http://washington.embassy.qa/en

Address: 2555 M St. NW, Washington, DC, 20037

Opening times:

Mon-Fri 09:00-17:00 (embassy business hours); 09:30-12:30 (consulate section)

Embassy of the State of Qatar in the UK

Telephone: +44 20 7493 2200

Website: http://london.embassy.qa/en/embassy

Address: Mayfair, 1 South Audley Street, London, W1K 1NB

Opening times:

Mon-Fri 09:30-16:00 (general enquiries); 10:00-13:00 (visa section)

British Embassy in Qatar

Telephone: +974 4496 2000

Website: https://www.gov.uk/world/organisations/bembassy-doha

Address: West Bay, Doha

Opening times:

Sun-Wed 08:00-15:30, Thurs 08:00-13:30

Qatar Health Care and Vaccinations

Title	Special Precautions
Diphtheria	Sometimes
Hepatitis A	Yes
Malaria	No
Rabies	Sometimes
Tetanus	Yes
Typhoid	Sometimes
Yellow Fever	No

Health Care

Excellent hospitals run by both the government and the commercial sector may be found in Qatar. Additionally, Doha is home to a sizable number of pharmacies with English-speaking employees. Despite this, travellers ought to carry travel insurance.

Food and Drink

In Doha and other urban places, drinking tap water is safe. Bottled water is a wise precaution in other places. It is acceptable to eat from markets and street food booths because, generally speaking, food cleanliness and standards are good. Only consume well-cooked meat and fish, and use common sense.

Other Risks

When temperatures reach 34°C (95°F) or above, tourists are most in danger of suffering from heat stroke. Simple precautions like covering the head, avoiding the noon heat, and drinking enough water can prevent this. Respiratory issues may also be brought on by sandstorms.

Certificate

Visitors who intend to stay for more than one month should undergo a medical examination, including HIV testing.

Qatar Public Holidays

Below are listed public holidays in Qatar

Eid al-Fitr (End of Ramadan)

01 May 2022

Eid al-Adha (Feast of Sacrifice)

09 July 2022

National Day

18 December 2022

Money and duty-free for Qatar

Currency and Money

Currency information

Qatar Riyal (QAR; symbol QR)=100 dirhams. Notes are in denominations of QR500, 100, 50, 10, 5 and 1. Coins are in denominations of 50, 25, 10, 5, and 1 dirhams. The information exchange rate is pegged to the US dollar at an average rate of US$1= QR3.64

Credit cards

American Express, Diners Club, MasterCard and Visa are widely accepted.

There are Automated Teller Machines throughout Qatar.

Traveller's cheques

Traveller's cheques are no longer popular

Banking hours

Sun-Thu 07:30-12:00 and 15:30-19:30

Currency restrictions

There are no restrictions on the import or export of local or foreign currency, but cash, precious jewellery and all financial means need to be declared if their value exceeds QR50,000. The Israeli currency is prohibited.

Currency exchange

All major banks and hotels will exchange currency

Qatar duty-free

Overview

The following goods may be imported into Qatar without incurring customs duty:

Cigarettes (alternatively 20 cigars or 300g pipe tobacco or 500g raw tobacco or 2kg Shisha hookah, as long as the value of the tobacco products does not exceed QR3,000).

Value of one gift below QR3,000

Please note that you cannot take alcohol with you.

Banned imports

Alcoholic drinks, drugs, indecent materials (books, magazines, etc), weapons, ammunition, explosives and radioactive equipment.

Doha Travel Guide

About Doha

Doha, the capital of Qatar, is fascinating, though thought-provoking and somewhat bizarre. It combines desert scenery with a futuristic skyline and more wealth than any other city in the world.

Its continuously expanding cityscape of avant-garde and ostentatious buildings shows that it is committed to becoming a major tourist destination to compete with its neighbours in the Emirates.

The grandiose intentions Doha has for its sister "Smart City," Lusail, will be realized in time for the 2022 World Cup.

There are plenty of activities to keep visitors entertained despite the city's lack of historical significance and enormous shopping complex.

Qatar makes up for its paucity of artefacts with a passion for the arts, and its rich coffers assist to fill its museums. The Katara cultural town, which features everything from art galleries to classical music recitals, is a special highlight.

At first glance, Dubai's expansive malls and sparkling skyline may appear to be more similar to that city than its more traditional Arabian neighbours. Qatar shares a lot of similarities with Saudi Arabia, which is the nation that borders it in the south, nevertheless.

Doha is a fascinating location because of its confluence of extreme religious conservatism and unrestrained consumerism. The glitzy new bars that are opening up in the western hotels are off-limits to Qatari women, regardless of whether they are wearing western or traditional attire. Friday, the most religious day of the week, is a bizarre combination of mosque attendance followed by shopping binges on Western labels and brands in the vast malls. Weekend "brunching" is now a well-liked weekend activity because of the thriving food industry.

While much of Doha is brand-new, some areas, like Souq Waqif, still have Arabian influences. Qataris go to this market to shop and eat, just as they have for the past 150 years.

Although it was rebuilt in the 1970s and is a favourite among tourists, its authenticity is unaffected. Locals buy birds for their favourite sport in the neighbouring Falconry Souk, but couples getting married still choose to visit the Gold Souk. This is where you can experience the multicultural, multifaceted, and both conservative and modern Doha.

Key facts

Population: 339,847

Latitude: 25.294632

Longitude: 51.507513

W Doha

The W brand is known for providing a little bit of Manhattan in the middle of the Middle East, so those who are familiar with it will know what to anticipate here. It is conveniently positioned and might be used by urban socialites who are fashion-conscious as well as business travellers. There are several excellent dining and nightlife options, and the design is slick and contemporary.

Four Seasons Hotel Doha

The Four Seasons is a good option for a quick getaway because it has one of Doha's top spas, spread out across three stories, and a private beach that gently curves. There are seven restaurants and lounges to choose from, and the pool areas are attractively landscaped. It is a luxurious hotel with first-rate service, lavish marble décor, and a surprisingly laid-back atmosphere. With a kids' club and family events, those with kids are adequately accommodated.

Meliã

This Spanish-owned hotel will more than satisfy those who want to blend in. The third-floor swimming pool provides a chic place to unwind and cool down, and the guest rooms are modern and roomy. Its best feature is the Sanjeev Kapoor award-winning signature restaurant. Aceite is another option if you want friendly service and sangria on tap. Visitors to this hotel have discounted access to Banana Island and Katara Beach.

Souq Waqif Boutique Hotels

This group of nine structures puts you right in the middle of Souq Waqif and gives you a true sense of Doha's ancient side. The hotel offers access to a variety of amenities, including a luxury spa with Arabic treatments (including a traditional hammam), eight restaurants, and a rooftop pool. It has an alluring Arabesque style and boutique vibe. 11 different room classifications, valet parking, and Qatari hospitality are further advantages.

The Torch Doha

The tallest hotel in Qatar is now this 300 m (984 ft) tower, which is a part of the city's high-tech Aspire Zone. Despite not being designed from the beginning as a hotel, it still provides outstanding levels of in-room comfort and some very impressive amenities. On travels during the warmer months, expect to rub shoulders with football players, while the nearby Villagio Mall features a Venice motif.

Warwick, Doha

This hotel has 164 rooms and suites with traditional Arabic design, meeting spaces, a rooftop pool, and a 335 square meter spa with steam and fitness rooms. It is conveniently located for accessing Downtown Doha's attractions. Particularly well-liked activities include dining at L'aubere and their Wednesday BBQ nights. There are comfortable spots to sit and take in the city views at Moon Deck and its Rooftop Grill.

Doha History

Even though Qatar is one of the richest nations in the world relative to its population, it was one of the poorest in the Middle East before the discovery of oil and natural gas in the middle of the 20th century.

The majority of Qataris depended on pearl or sea fishing for their livelihood, and up until the early 1970s, the nation had spent centuries travelling between several occupying powers.

Sheikh Than Bin Muhammed was made Sheikh of Qatar in 1825 by the Ottomans, who at the time ruled the majority of Arabia. Since then, the Al Thani family has been in charge of Qatar, which is still an absolute monarchy, despite having been ruled first by the Ottomans and then by the British Protectorate when the Turks departed from Doha in 1916.

During the 75 years of the British Protectorate Agreement, Doha and other Gulf cities experienced severe economic hardship. Despite the discovery of oil and natural gas deposits, the pearl fishing sector faltered as the Japanese cultured pearl industry expanded, and many Qataris lived in abject poverty. Britain's engagement in World War II distracted it from its concerns about the Middle East, allowing Qatar to sulk in a decade of economic doldrums.

Production of oil and gas started in 1949, and by the 1960s, Doha was among the richest cities in the area. Due to the conservatism of the ruling Emir, the country remained largely undeveloped and as the period as an English Protectorate began to draw to a close, Qatar agreed to join the other eight states (the present-day UAE and Bahrain) to form a union of Arab Emirates.

The nine states had yet to agree on the duration of the Union when the Protectorate ended in 1971. On September 3, 1971, Qatar withdrew and declared its independence, designating Doha as its capital.

In a bloodless coup in 1995, the deputy emir Sheikh Hamad bin Khalifa ousted his father and is widely credited with advancing democracy and open society in the nation. It is currently a very affluent nation, and it is anticipated that in the future, it will draw more and more attention.

Did you know?

The first hospital in Doha didn't open until 1947. Before this, Qataris had to travel abroad to receive medical care.

The Al Bidda Park in the city is being excavated to reveal the ruins of a late 18th-century village.

A former ruler who was ordered to pay a fine to the British for encouraging piracy in the 19th century was unable to come up with the money and was instead given a booth with silver and gold jewellery as well as two blades.

Weather in Doha

Doha enjoys year-round sunshine due to its arid desert climate, yet during the hot season, you might wish to avoid the sun and the sweltering heat (May to October).

The cool season, which lasts from November to March, is the ideal time to visit Doha. The daily average temperature is 25°C (77°F) in November and drops to 18°C (64°F) in January, which is also the coldest month. Doha receives just 75mm (3 in) of rain annually, and it also falls throughout this time.

May to October is the hot season, which is extremely hot and muggy. With an average high temperature of 42°C (108°F) and the potential to reach a sweltering 50°C (122°F) on some days, July is frequently the hottest month. The hot season is not conducive to sightseeing. After July, temperatures begin to gradually decrease, however, travellers may still find the heat unpleasant. The average maximum temperature by October is 35°C (95°F), but after that, it begins to cool off.

About Doha Hamad International Airport (DOH)

The Gulf State of Qatar is served by the Doha Hamad International Airport. This Doha Hamad International Airport directory offers contact information for the airport as well as information on getting to and from the airport, terminal amenities, and surrounding lodging alternatives.

Information:

Information desks are situated in the Arrivals Meet and Greet Hall and immediately inside the entrance of the Departures Check-in-Hall.

Website:

https://www.dohahamdairport.com

Driving directions:

From central Qatar, it is easy to find the airport. To get to the Ras Abboud Expressway, take Al Corniche Street east, then turn left onto Ras Abboud Road. Turn left at the roundabout onto the F Ring Road after travelling for around 5 km (3 miles), which will take you right up to the terminal door.

Airport info:

Code: DOH

Address: Doha Hamad International Airport, Doha

Location: The airport is located around 9km (5.6 miles) southeast of central Doha.

Number of terminals: 1

Telephone: +974 4010 6666

Time Zone: Arabia Standard Time GMT +0300

Public Transport

Public transport road:

Bus: The regular Mowasalat bus routes 109 and 747 (tel. +974 4458 8588; website: www.mowasalat.com) go into the city from the Bus Pavilion, which is to the right of the Arrivals Hall. The Doha Bus Station and Doha Hamad International Airport both have ticket vending machines where customers can acquire an electronic "Karwa" Smartcard for payment. The "Limited" version of the card costs QR10 and is good for two trips within 24 hours of purchase. Within 24 hours of purchase, the QR20 "Infinite" card entitles the holder to an unlimited number of trips across the city.

Taxi: There are plenty of taxis (also run by the state-owned Mowasalat) waiting outside the arrivals hall at the Taxi Pavilion. The basic fare for taxis is QR 25, and they are all metered. The trip into the city centre takes no more than 20 minutes. It should be noted that only cash in Qatari Riyals is accepted as payment. A limousine service is also provided by the same business.

Call Mowasalat in advance (tel: +974 4458 8888) to reserve a taxi that is appropriate for people with impaired mobility (PRM).

Terminal facilities

Money:

In the airport, there are numerous ATMs and bureaux de change. To locate the closest ATM or money exchange office, follow the signs or ask at the information desk. On the lower level of the arrivals hall is where you'll find the Water Islamic Bank (QIB).

Food:

There is a good selection of eateries throughout the airport, including an American diner and an Italian restaurant, that provide food that is both regionally and internationally inspired.

Shopping:

A sizable area of the Doha Hamad International Airport is designated for duty-free shopping. In the primary shopping area between concourses A and B, D and E, there are dozens of stores. Luxury goods, electronics, fashion, cosmetics, and jewellery are among the products that these stores specialize in.

Luggage:

At the airport, there is also a service for lost items. If your luggage was misplaced during the flight, get in touch with Qatar Aviation Services at +974 4462 6531 or llqas@qataraviation.com. If it was misplaced at the passenger terminal, get in touch with the airport centre at +984 4010 6666 or hialostproperty@hamadairport.com.qa

Other:

Additional facilities found within the terminal include prayer rooms, baby changing facilities, children's play areas and designated smoking rooms.

Airport facilities

Conference and business:

There are a variety of conference and meeting rooms accessible at larger hotels in the centre, however, there are no meeting facilities at the airport. The Oryx Rotana Hotel (tel. +974 4402 3333; www.rotana.com) and the Crowne Plaza Doha (tel. +974 4408 7777; www.crowneplaza.com) are the ones closest to the airport. The distance between these two and Doha Hamad International Airport is roughly 20 minutes. There is a business centre in the airport, which is accessible to premium travellers for free or for a small price, and it is situated in the Oryx Lounge.

Communication facilities:

Unlimited free Wi-Fi access is available everywhere in the airport, and there are additional free internet kiosks at various locations. Public telephones (using prepaid cards) are placed throughout the terminal.

Disabled facilities:

With elevators, ramps, walkways, and disabled restrooms, the airport is completely accessible to passengers with disabilities. There are designated disability parking places in both the short-term and long-term parking lots. Long-term parking is located at the southern end of the passenger terminal, while short-term parking is on either side of the terminal. Both provide parking under cover. If a passenger thinks they might need more help, they should get in touch with the airline before their trip.

Car parking:

Long-term parking is located at the southern end of the passenger terminal, while short-term parking is on either side of the terminal. Additionally accessible and appropriate for passengers flying with Qatar Airways is a premium parking lot. Parking costs can be found at dohahamadairport.com.

Car rental:

Numerous international and local operators are represented at the airport, and servant ice counters can be found across the Arrivals Hall in the passenger terminal.

Doha Hamad International Airport Hotels

Luxury

Crowne Plaza Doha

The Crowne Plaza Doha West Bay welcomes you to a new and improved way to conduct business travel. It is situated in Doha's prestigious West Bay neighbourhood located 20 kilometres from the Hamad International Airport, 15 minutes from the Souq Waqif and Museum, and 1.4 kilometres from the Doha Exhibition & Convention Center, this contemporary hotel with 317 rooms gives visitors quick access to Qatar's commercial, diplomatic, and financial districts. a short drive from the Doha City Center Mall, the Corniche promenade, eateries, and the greatest nightlife.

When attending the Formula 1 Grand Prix and Arab Cup 2021, the hotel is the ideal home away from home because of its convenient location near Lusail International Circuit and easy access to Qatar's football stadiums.

The contemporary decor, variety of restaurants, and spa at Crowne Plaza Doha West Bay will wow even the most sophisticated tourist as you take in the city's striking cityscape.

Nidaaya Restaurant

On the sixth level of the hotel, Nidaaya serves a delectable breakfast. It provides international cuisines in a chic and energetic setting. The restaurant offers a wide range of international delicacies and features live cooking stations.

Guest Room and Suites

Address: Airport Road, Doha

Telephone: +974 4408 7777

Website: http://www.ihg.com

Oryx Rotana Hotel

The Oryx Rotana is a luxurious establishment with several restaurants, an outdoor pool, and a massage parlour that is only a short drive from the airport and only a few minutes from the city centre. On-site meeting spaces are also available for professional use.

Guest room and suite

Swimming Pool Hyatt Regency Onyx Doha

Address: Al Matar Street, Doha

Telephone: +974 4402 3333

Website: http://www.rotana.com

Oryx Airport Hotel

The Airport Hotel, which is inside the passenger terminal, provides transiting guests with stays as short as three hours and a variety of hotel types, including larger luxury suites. There is dining available, as well as a "wellness centre" with a pool and a gym.

Guest Room and Suites

Doha Airpot Lounge

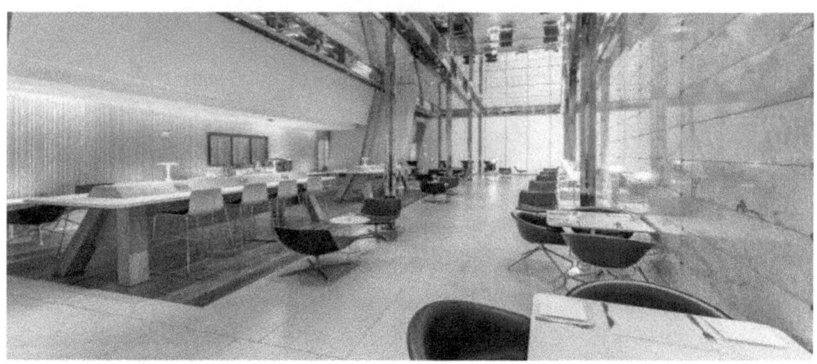

Address: Doha Hamad International Airport, Doha

Telephone: +974 4010 8100

Website: http://oryxairporthotel.com/

Qatar World Cup 2022 – in numbers

Teams: 32

Playing venues: 8

Matches: 65

Opening match: Al Bayt Stadium

Final: Lusail Stadium

Average venue capacity: 47,500 seats

Largest venue: Lusail Stadium (80,000 seats)

Smallest venue: Multiple venues (40,000 seats)

Average no. of matches per venue: 8.1

1. Lusail

Lusail Stadium |

Capacity: 80,000 seats |

Opening: 2022

Matches:

5x Group Matches

1x Round of 16

1x Quarter-Final

1x Semi-Final

Final

2. Al Khor

Al Bayt Stadium |

Capacity: 60,000 seats |

Opening: 2021

Matches:

5x Group Matches (incl. Opening Match)

1x Round of 16

1x Quarter-Final

1x Semi-Final

3. Al Wakrah

Al Janoub Stadium |

Capacity: 40,000 seats |

Opening: 2019

Matches:

5x Group Matches

1x Round of 16

4. Al Rayyan

Ahmad Bin Ali Stadium |

Capacity: 40,000 seats |

Opening: 2020

Matches:

5x Group Matches

1x Round of 16

5. Doha

Khalifa International Stadium |

Capacity: 40,000 seats |

Opening: 1976

Matches:

5x Group Matches

1x Round of 16

Match for Third Place

6. Doha

Education City Stadium |

Capacity: 40,000 seats |

Opening: 2020

Matches:

5x Group Matches

1x Round of 16

1x Quarter-Final

7. Doha

Stadium 974 |

Capacity: 40,000 seats |

Opening: 2021

Matches:

5x Group Matches

1x Round of 16

8. Doha

Al Thumama Stadium |

Capacity: 40,000 seats |

Opening: 2021

Matches:

5x Group Matches

1x Round of 16

1x Quarter-Final

www.ingramcontent.com/pod-product-compliance
Lightning Source LLC
LaVergne TN
LVHW050340160826
845677LV00014B/3707

* 9 7 9 8 8 4 7 4 3 0 1 1 1 *